Assessing the quality of open and distance learning materials

Alan Clarke

THE NATIONAL ORGANISATION
FOR ADULT LEARNING

Department for Education and Employment

Published by the National Institute of Adult Continuing Education
(England and Wales)
21 De Montfort Street, Leicester LE1 7GE
Company registration no. 2603322
Charity registration no. 1002775

The NIACE website on the internet is http://www.niace.org.uk

First published 2001
© NIACE

CATALOGUING IN PUBLICATIONS DATA
A CIP record of this title is available from the British Library
ISBN 1 86201 119 2

Typeset by Boldface, London
Cover design by Boldface, London
Printed in Great Britain by Russell Press

Contents

Acknowledgements

I would like to thank my colleagues in NIACE for their continued support and all the organisations taking part in the Adult and Community Learning and Laptops initiative. The Department for Education and Employment for their continued support. Lisa Englebright for her helpful comments on the content of the package and Vivienne Rivis of Bradford and Ilkley College for her suggestions in turning an idea into practice. I would also like to thank Fiona Aldridge, Jackie Essom and Ewa Rawicka for their helpful comments.

Introduction

Almost all learning involves the use of learning materials in some way. They may be designed and produced by an individual tutor, be commercially developed for thousands of learners, be informal (e.g. a good book) or simply a friend's notes who has already completed the course. This guide is intended to help the use, design and selection of appropriate open and distance learning materials. It assumes that you will be using the materials as part of a flexible learning programme. Open and distance learning can take a wide variety of forms and contexts so that you will need to judge when the guidance is appropriate. It will not be applicable in all situations. A package that works well in one situation or context may fail in another.

What are open and distance learning materials?

Open and distance learning materials can take many forms. They can include:

- Workbooks – a set of exercises which the learners work through on their own but normally with tutorial support in the room or nearby;

- Structured materials – these are studied remotely from the tutor but with some form of communication link such as a telephone number, e-mail address or occasional face-to-face meetings;

- Computer-based training (CBT) – there are often specific packages aimed at helping the learner to develop skills and knowledge in relation to a defined task or subject (e.g. answering the telephone, customers relations, accounts procedures etc.). CBT is often designed to be self-contained with little or no outside support;

- Online materials – these are materials accessed over the World Wide Web. They can take a variety of forms from resources presented on a website to interactive multimedia;

- Audio and video can also be used as ways of making distance learning a more personalised and less isolating experience. In this country these are specifically generated for large groups studying the same material to make it cost effective. However, in Australia, for example, where distance learning is part of education for all there are special facilities available for the tutors to record short video and audio cassettes where it is felt it will benefit the students. This is especially important in areas such as languages and the arts.

Quality issues

Learners

When you are assessing the quality and suitability of learning materials there are several fundamental issues to consider:

- who is the material designed for?

- who are the learners?

- how long will it take learners to study the whole package and each section?

- is there a clear explanation of any study timetable that has to be followed?

- what will learners be able to do, know and understand by the end of the package?

Who is the material designed for?
Good materials have been developed for a specific group or groups of learners. It has been customised to meet their precise needs. The material should clearly state who it is aimed at.

What is the target group of learners?
The target group of learners should be defined in terms of their existing experience, knowledge and skills. Who will benefit from using these materials? It should be clearly stated.

Example:
The package assumes that you have some experience of using a computer in that you are able to:

- use a mouse and keyboard to interact with computer software;
- load an application;
- save a file;
- print a document.

How long will it take the learner to study the material?
The material should indicate the time that it will take a learner to study the contents. Ideally this should be broken down section by section. This will help the learner plan their use of the package.

What will learners be able to do, know and understand after studying the package?
The material should state what the learning aims and objectives of the package are. This should be in terms of what the learner will be able to do after studying the package. This should be for the whole content and each separate section.

Example:
By the end of this chapter you should:

- feel more confident;
- understand the physical structure of a computer;
- be able to use a mouse;
- be able to use a keyboard;
- understand the components of the Windows 95 operating system.

How best to use the material?
It is good practice to provide learners with advice about how to study the material. This may take many forms including a study guide, guidance about how to plan their study or suggestions on how to cope with the assessment process.

How is the material delivered to the learner?
Often open and distance courses present learners with a large volume of material at the start of a course. This can be daunting to a new learner who may feel overwhelmed. It is important that materials are clearly

presented so learners can quickly and easily organise them and know where to start.

What are the hidden costs of using the materials?

Does the material require an significant extra costs from learners or the organisation (e.g. online costs for searches, attendance at residential conferences, and so on)?

Flexibility

How flexible is the material?

A key element of any open and distance learning package is that it should provide the learners and their tutors with some choice about how to use the package. The pack should allow the learners to:

- select which parts of the material to study;
- leave out sections which they already know and understand;
- select their own route through the material;
- learn in small logical chunks;
- understand how the different chunks fit together.

It should also allow a tutor to be able to customise the material to meet the local needs of learners.

Assessment

How will learners be assessed?

The material should clearly state how the learner will be assessed. The methods of assessment need to be stated in a straightforward style so the learner knows from the start of the course what is expected of them. Assistance can take a variety of forms but an assignment timetable, specimen answers, plain English explanation of deadlines, examinations and rules and a guide to the marking scheme are all helpful to the learner.

What forms of assessment are included in the package?

There are many different ways of assessing material. These include:

- pre-testing – it is good practice to provide an initial assessment to help the learner identify what they should study. In computer-based learning materials pre-tests can be used to customise the content to individual learners (e.g. to change the structure so that only material they do not already understand are presented to the learner);

- post-testing – it is again good practice to provide a final assessment so that learners are aware of what they have learned;

- portfolio – for many open learning packages learners are asked to develop a portfolio of evidence to show their competence or keep a learning diary.

Does the material help the learners to assess themselves?

Effective learning materials should help the learner to assess their own progress. This can take many forms but is closely related to the quality of the feedback.

Example:

1. **Computer-based materials** – feedback should build on the question and answer and not be limited to 'Well done' or 'Sorry that is not correct, have another go'.

   Better practice would be: 'Well done, the key issues are related to the location of the learning event because…' and 'Sorry that is not correct, consider what would influence the learner in their choice of event and then have another go…'

2. **Workbook** – questions should be followed by a discussion about the answer so the learner can judge their own answer against it. This helps them to assess their own progress.

3. **Content** – although it may seem obvious, check that the learning content covers the assessment questions (i.e. the assessment is not expecting the learners to answer questions not covered by the material).

Learning design

How does the material motivate the learner?

It is critical that the material will motivate your learners. This is difficult to assess in that it depends on both the subject and the learners' reasons for studying the material. However, it is worth considering:

- **language** – is the use of language appropriate to the learners? (e.g. a minimum of jargon with technical terms explained);

- **flexibility** – how flexible is the material? Does it give the learners a degree of choice?;

- **culture and background** – is the material suitable and motivating? Does the material allow for cultural diversity?

- **learning style** – does the material allow for learners having a range of preferred learning styles? That is, does the material use text and illustrations to explain the subject and allow them to:
  - reflect on what they are studying?;
  - understand the whole picture (i.e. wholist learning style)?;
  - understand the component parts (i.e. analytical learning style)?

- **learning strategy** – does the material help learners to employ a range of learning strategies?

- **structure** – does the material allow the learner to select what order to study the content, to stop and start (e.g. allow bookmarking in computer-based learning) where they want? Is the material divided into comfortable chunks for learning?

- **active** – does the design encourage the learners to be engaged actively in the material?

- **reinforcement** – does design aid the reinforcement of the learning (e.g. summaries, reviews, exercises to apply the material, etc)?

Is content appropriate for the learners, subject and level?
This needs both learners and tutors to judge. It is important to ask typical learners what their view of the material is and also to gain the views of experienced tutors.

Learner support

How does the learning material support the learner?
Almost all forms of open and distance learning material need some form of support. This can take many forms such as:

- within the material (e.g. answers to questions, discussion of answers, links to other sources, etc);
- tutor support (e.g. face-to-face, telephone, e-mail, chat rooms, etc);
- peer support (e.g. study group/circle).

The package should explain what support the design assumes (e.g. tutorial support, learning within group, etc). This is vital in that it determines the learning materials suitability in your environment. Could you provide tutorial support, organise peer learning groups, etc?

Learning strategies

What learning strategy does the material employ?
A well-designed learning package will be built around a distinct learning strategy. This should be apparent during your review of the material. If no approach is obvious then it probably is not systematically designed material and may not be effective.
An effective learning strategy will:

- motivate learners;
- encourage active learning;
- provide exercises, activities and self-assessment;
- assist learners to reflect on what they are studying and their previous learning experience;
- reinforce earlier learning;
- provide feedback.

Presentation

How is the material presented?

The first thing a learner or tutor will notice about a pack is how it is presented (e.g. colour, size (A4, A5, etc), binding, illustrations, etc). The appearance is important in that it can either motivate a learner to read and study its contents or make them reject the material. Most people will be unwilling to use a pack which is poorly presented. They will relate presentation to the quality of the learning.

How are illustrations used?

Illustrations can serve many purposes including:

- motivation;
- information;
- examples.

It is good practice to link and cross-reference clearly any illustrations to the text. An illustration, which is not linked to the text, will not aid learning. Illustrations can take many forms such as realistic images of objects being discussed in the text; charts, graphs and diagrams to provide information relating to the text; and analogies which are intended to help learners make a connection between the topics being discussed and their previous experience.

How suitable is the material for a wide range of learners?

The material should reflect that we are living in a multi-cultural and diverse society. It is important that the material does not portray stereotypes.

Computer-based learning materials

How are computer-based learning materials different from paper-based materials?
There are significant differences between paper-based and computer-based learning materials. In order to assess the quality and suitability of computer-based products it is important to consider additional factors.

How do learners interact with the material?
The major advantage of computer-based learning materials is that learners are able to interact with the content, so that it adapts to their needs, reactions and responses. If the material is essentially an electronic book you should consider if an actual book would have been a better choice. Many learners find reading a lot of information on a screen unpleasant so if that is all computer-based learning material provides, it is probably not going to achieve enormous results.

A key feature of good material is that the feedback provided to the learners is meaningful, detailed, appropriate and motivating.

How do learners navigate through the material?
There are several ways of structuring computer-based learning materials. These include:

- menus;
- hypertext;
- Graphical User Interface (GUI)

The important issue is that learners are able to:

- exit from the material at any point without too many steps;
- bookmark where they are so they can return next time to the same place;
- find easily what they are seeking;
- locate the information they are seeking because the structure, layout and presentation are consistent.

Learners should have a large degree of choice about which route to take when using the material. This should include not completing sections, repeating others and retaking tests. The learner should have the maximum degree of freedom.

How are the different media employed within the material?
Computer-based learning material can employ multiple media (e.g. video, sound, text, colour, still images, etc) so it is important to consider if they are used appropriately.

Examples:
- Video is effective in showing human interaction. Learners need to be given control over the playing of the video so that they can review the sequence or choose not to watch the sequence. It is often good practice to keep video sequences short.
- Animation is useful in showing things difficult to see another way (e.g. microscopic).
- Colour is motivating if not over-used where it can confuse and irritate.
- Pictures are motivating and can present considerable content if integrated with the text.
- Sound can irritate so that learners need to be able to control the volume and switch it off.

How easy is it to install the material?
This is a fundamental requirement of the material so the package should be accompanied by straightforward guidance on the hardware it requires and how to install the package.

What support does the supplier provide?
It is important that the supplier is able to provide you with help with technical problems in a straightforward way (e.g. telephone help line).

Evaluation methods

In principle you should never buy an open learning product without evaluating it. However, evaluation can take many forms. Some possible approaches are:

- Independent reviews of material – some material is reviewed in a similar way to book reviews. This is not usually enough evidence to support a decision to buy the product but probably enough to consider it;

- Expert review is an important approach to evaluation. A single expert can provide a lot of evidence about the design, content and viability of open and distance learning materials;

- Learners – an expert cannot provide you with a learner's viewpoint and it is important to consider how learners will react to the product.

An effective approach is probably layered in that you will not wish to invest too much time in a product that you are not sure about. The initial layer is for a subject expert to review the material to assess if an evaluation is worthwhile. Once this decision has been made then an effective evaluation should include:

- Learners – three or four learners will provide you with a comprehensive analysis of a package;

- Expert – a single expert will be able to assess the design, assessment and content of the product;

- A framework for the evaluators to ensure a consistent and systematic approach. See 'Checklist Evaluation of Learning Materials', pages 25-26.

For computer-based learning products there are some additional factors which include:

- Installing the software – how easy or difficult is the process? Could a tutor or learner install it or do you need a Technician?

- Software failure – is it easy to crash by deliberately getting things wrong in the same way a group of learners might behave?

- Is the package effective on computers of different specification?

- Is the feedback and remedial help for each assessment question effective?

Techniques

There are many techniques that can be used to evaluate materials. However, three main techniques are often employed. These are:

- Interviewing
- Questionnaires
- Observation

Interviewing

Interviewing learners or expert users can take several forms. The main options being:

- Structured – that is, all the questions are agreed in advance and simply asked and the answers recorded. This is easy to undertake and requires relatively little interviewing expertise. It is suitable when you are absolutely certain what you want to know. The answers from this type of interview are easier to analyse since they are all based on the same questions.

- Open – that is, all the questions are decided during the interview to respond to the answers given by the subject. In this type of interview you are trying to probe the knowledge and views of the interviewees. This approach is suitable when you are unsure of what you need to discover. This type of interviewing technique requires a skilled interviewer with considerable expertise. The answers from this type of interview are difficult to analyse since all the questions are different.

- Semi-structured – this is a combination of structured and open interviewing techniques. It allows you to combine the advantages of both approaches. Standard questions can provide a framework for the interview and the interviewer is given the freedom to follow up answers that they judge to be interesting. The answers are easier to analyse than a purely open interview in that there is a partial structure and all questions, even those which are follow-ups, are related to standard ones.

Questionnaires

Questionnaires are based on two types of question. These are:

- Open questions – these are ones which require a response other than yes or no. These types of question provide a rich source of information. However, quite often they are poorly answered and even when they are answered well it is difficult to analyse due to the range of responses

- Closed questions – these require an answer based on the subject making a choice between options, such as yes or no

Example:
A useful way of combining open and closed questions is to provide the subject with a range of choices such as:

How interactive did you judge the package?

Highly   Reasonably   Poor   Not Interactive

Circle all options that apply

I have used: CD-ROM
                      Internet
                      E-mail
                      Chat

These types of questions are straightforward to analyse but do not reveal the individual's ideas or experience in any real depth.

Observation

Observing learners using a package can be very informative. However, being watched is often a distraction for the individual so their behaviour may not be typical. Usually you need to let the people being observed get used to your presence so that eventually you merge into the background. This can take a little time so it is good practice to do several sessions of observation.

It is probably impossible to select a viewing position that allows you to see everything or to be able to observe all the individual's behaviour. Before you start, decide what the key factors are that you are interested in and concentrate on them. It is difficult to make notes and observe, so design a recording sheet with the key factors marked. This will help you to make rapid notes.

A useful approach that enhances observing is to encourage the individual to speak out loud. This technique is widely used in evaluating software and can be very effective with computer-based learning. The observer can assess the learner's behaviour and the individual's own comments help the observer to know what they are thinking. Some people are very good at providing a commentary while others may need to practise.

Cost-effectiveness

The cost of open learning follows a different pattern to conventional learning courses. The key costs associated with open and distance learning are:

- Cost of learning materials;
- Learning Centre costs;
- People costs – mentor, tutor, learning centre staff, etc;
- Assessment costs;
- Equipment;
- Telephone, lease line costs, etc;
- Administration costs;
- Travel costs and time for face-to-face meetings.

Cost-effectiveness is not simply about the actual costs but also an assessment of the benefits of open and distance learning. This includes:

- Flexibility – does it allow many learners to take part who would be excluded by conventional approaches (e.g. fixed class times):
  - Learning not restricted by location;
  - Learning not restricted by pace of learning;
  - Learning not restricted by time of course.

- Availability – allows a wider range of learning to be provided;

- Removes or reduces learners travel time and costs.

Cost-effectiveness needs to balance costs with the benefits/advantages that open and distance learning provides. Two simple models are often suggested.

These are:

1. providing a flexible learning programme for learners who would not normally be able to access learning. This is maximising the benefits of open and distance learning for a relatively small group of learners. This often requires the tailoring of material to meet the needs of a target group.

2. Providing a large-scale programme for many learners in a single subject (e.g. accounts technician, computer literacy or GCSE). By providing a large programme the unit cost is relatively low so it is cost-effective. This is the opposite of option 1 in that a standard programme is provided rather than a customised one.

Commission a bespoke supplier

You are occasionally going to employ a third party company to develop learning materials on your behalf. Some of the issues you should consider when undertaking this task are:

- Financial stability – you want to be sure that whoever you are doing business with is not going to go bankrupt and leave you in the lurch. Ask to see their accounts for a year or two. Who owns the company? How long have they been established?

- Expertise – ask them for:
  - details of other work they have carried out;
  - examples of packages produced;
  - references from other customers;
  - CVs of staff demonstrating their ability and experience in learning design, graphic design, and computer skills;
  - what support can they provide (e.g. help line);
  - their approach to design and development ;
  - their approach to quality assurance.

A common weakness of learning materials and, in particular, computer-based learning packages is that they are not designed to maximise learning. Consider quality issues discussed earlier and use them as a basis to evaluate examples provided and as an aid to interviewing suppliers or during visits to their offices.

Licences

All open and distance learning materials are accompanied by a licence which defines how the material can be used. The licence may simply stop you copying the material or provide you with a licence to photocopy the material although this is often restricted to using it for educational purposes within your organisation (i.e. registered students).

You need to study the licence before you buy any learning material but computer-based products need considering in detail. Software licences often limit the number of simultaneous learners that can study the material. The cost of computer-based learning packages is often determined by the number of simultaneous learners it will support. You may be offered:

- An individual licence;
- Up to five learners;
- Up to 100 learners;
- A site licence (i.e. unlimited learners on a single site).

The price of the package increases with the number of learners. However, many suppliers will negotiate and offer discounts for educational establishments.

Checklist evaluation of learning materials

The key features to consider in reviewing material of all types are given below:

1. Who are the materials designed for?

2. When was the material published (is it up-to-date)?

3. What will your learners be able to do after studying the material?

4. What will your learners know after studying the material?

5. What advice does the material offer the learner to help their studies?

6. What does the material assume the learner knows already?

7. What mixture of media does the material use (e.g. video, text, sound, animation, and so on)?

8. Is the material going to motivate your learners?

9. What support does the package assume learners will need?

10. How are the materials presented?
    - Are they written in plain English?
    - Are they easy to navigate?
    - Do they feel high quality?
    - Are illustrations used to support the text?
    - Is the learner able to choose what to learn and what to leave out?
    - Are the materials broken down in order to aid learning?

11. Do the materials encourage active learning?

12. Are you able to identify a clear structure that will aid learning?

13. How is the learner assessed? Does the material relate to a qualification?

14. Where does the material assume the learner is studying (e.g. at home, at work, in a learning centre)?

In addition to these general criteria for computer-based learning materials you should also consider:

15. What hardware and software do you require to use the product?

16. What supporting material is provided (in print or on the screen)? Is it clearly presented and readily available?

17. How easy is the package to install?

18. What are the licence requirements (e.g. does it allow you to use on more than one computer at a time)?

19. How easy is it to use the material (e.g. do you need to an expert computer user)?

20. What technical help does the supplier offer?

Many suppliers will provide you with a review copy of their materials for a short period to help you decide if you want to buy it. Always return the material within the agreed time period or be prepared to pay for them. Suppliers will frequently invoice you automatically if you keep the materials longer than the agreed review period. It is important to involve learners, tutors and support staff in the evaluation process.

Useful contacts

Basic Skills Agency
http://www.basic-skills.org.uk
Commonwealth House,
1-19 New Oxford Street,
London WC1A 1NU
Tel. 020 7405 4017

British Association of Open Learning
http://www.baol.co.uk
Suite 12, Pixmore Centre,
Pixmore Avenue,
Letchworth,
Hertfordshire SG6 1JG.
Tel. 01462 485588.
Fax. 01462 485633

British Educational and Communication Technology Agency
http://www.becta.org.uk

Department for Education and Employment
http://www.dfee.gov.uk

The Institute for Computer Based Learning
http://www.icbl.hw.ac.uk
Heriot Watt University
EH14 4AS

The Institute of IT Training
Institute House,
University of Warwick Science Park,
Coventry CV4 7EZ.
Tel: 01203 418128.

Learning and Skills Development Agency
Citadel Place,
Tinworth Street,
London SE 11 5EH

National Institute of Adult Continuing Education
http://www.niace.org.uk
21 De Montfort Street,
Leicester, LE1 7GE.
Tel. 0116 204 4200.

Qualifications and Curriculum Authority
http://www.qca.org.uk
29 Bolton Street,
London W1Y 7PD

Technologies for Training
http://www.tft.co.uk

Ufi
http://www.ufiltd.co.uk

World Association for Online Education
http://www.waoe.org
Calder, J (1994)
Programme Evaluation and Quality,
Kogan Page

Useful publications

Clarke, A and Walmsley, J (1999)
Open Learning Materials and Learning Centres
NIACE

Clarke, A (2001)
Designing Computer-based Learning
Gower

Hunt, M and Clarke, A (1999)
A Guide to the Cost Effectiveness of Technology Based Training, Department for Education and Employment
London

Lockitt, B (1999)
Right tools for the job: evaluating multimedia, flexibility and open learning materials
Further Education and Development Agency, London

Oppenheim, L (2000)
Questionnaire Design
Continuum International Publishing Group

Rae, L (1997)
Evaluation Approaches for Training and Development
Kogan Page

Rowntree, D (1990)
Exploring Open and distance Learning
The Open University

Rowntree, D (1990)
Teaching Through Self-Instruction: How to Develop Open Learning materials
Kogan Page

Thorpe, M (1993)
Evaluating Open and Distance Learning
Longman